DINOSAURS
A to Z

DINOSAURS
A to Z

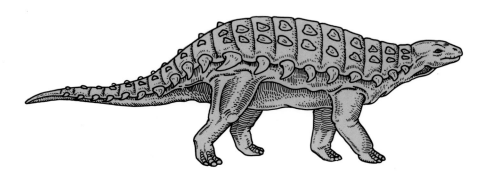

Joseph Wallace

Illustrations by Robert Frank

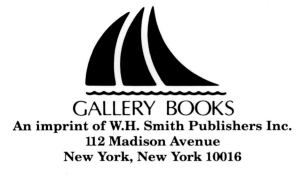

GALLERY BOOKS
An imprint of W.H. Smith Publishers Inc.
112 Madison Avenue
New York, New York 10016

A FRIEDMAN GROUP BOOK

Published by GALLERY BOOKS
An imprint of W.H. Smith Publishers, Inc.
112 Madison Avenue
New York, New York 10016

ISBN 0-8317-2296-7

DINOSAURS A TO Z
was prepared and produced by
Michael Friedman Publishing Group, Inc.
15 West 26th Street
New York, NY 10010

Designer: David B. Weisman
Photography Editor: Christopher Bain
Production Manager: Karen L. Greenberg

Macintosh output by Line & Tone Typografix Corp.
Color separations by Universal Colour Scanning, Ltd.
Printed and bound in Hong Kong by Leefung-Asco Printers, Ltd.

Gallery Books are available for bulk purchase for sales promotions and premium use.
For details write or telephone the Manager of Special Sales, W.H. Smith Publishers, Inc.,
112 Madison Avenue, New York, New York 10016. (212) 532-6600

Illustrator's Dedication:
To my wife, Pat,
and my mother, Dory,
for their love and support

Introduction:

What is it about the dinosaurs?

What makes them such enduring objects of our fascination and enthusiasm? Such popular subjects for books, movies, and toys? Such an exciting field for research, despite the fact that they've been extinct for millions of years?

Ask paleontologists, the scientists who study dinosaurs, and you're likely to get some mumbled explanation about the power of the imagination. Ask children, and they'll tell you how cool it is that such huge animals once stalked the earth. Then both groups will look at you and say, "Who knows?"

One thing that keeps the dinosaurs in the public eye is that they are constantly surprising us. For many years after their discovery in the early 1800s, most experts thought that the dinosaurs were stupid, slow-moving, cold-blooded creatures that died out as soon as something better (like the mammals) came along.

But in recent years, paleontologists have made dozens of important discoveries that contradict these and other long-held theories. Dinosaur nests, eggs (some unbroken and containing fossilized embryos), footprints, and hundreds of thousands of bones from every continent on earth (even Antarctica) have taught us that the dinosaurs were far more complicated and fascinating than we imagined even a decade ago.

We now know, for example, that the dinosaurs were intelligent enough to dominate all life on earth for 160 million years, far longer than any other animal. From humid lowland swamps to piny mountaintops, the great reptiles roamed all over the ancient continents. Mammals, birds, and other creatures that shared the planet with the dinosaurs stayed out of their way, much as smaller animals avoid contact with humans, the dominant animals on earth today.

Dinosaurs were also far from the shambling, creeping creatures that they've long been described as. Some types (such as the meat-eating *Velociraptor*) could run as fast as a racehorse, and even the hulking

© Gregory S. Paul

Above: This painting of a hyperactive *Dilophosaurus* is a perfect example of how most scientists now believe that dinosaurs were agile, fast-moving creatures.

Right: Footprints, like this one left by a *Dilophosaurus* more than 150 million years ago, can tell scientists a great deal about the way dinosaurs lived.

Stegosaurus and *Apatosaurus* could move faster than a human can today. In fact, fascinating studies have shown that many of the dinosaurs were remarkably agile, and energetic—so much so that many scientists believe that they may have been warm-blooded, like mammals and birds.

Dinosaur hunters have also uncovered fascinating new evidence about how the great reptiles lived. Whereas most modern reptiles lay their eggs and then abandon them, *Maiasaura*, and almost certainly other dinosaurs, seem to have been caring parents. They built nests in colonies, guarded their eggs, and brought food back to their babies, habits that again closely resemble those of today's birds and mammals.

All this similarity between birds and dinosaurs shouldn't be surprising, since we've long known that the two are closely related. *Archaeopteryx*, first discovered more than a century ago, was a dinosaur that clearly

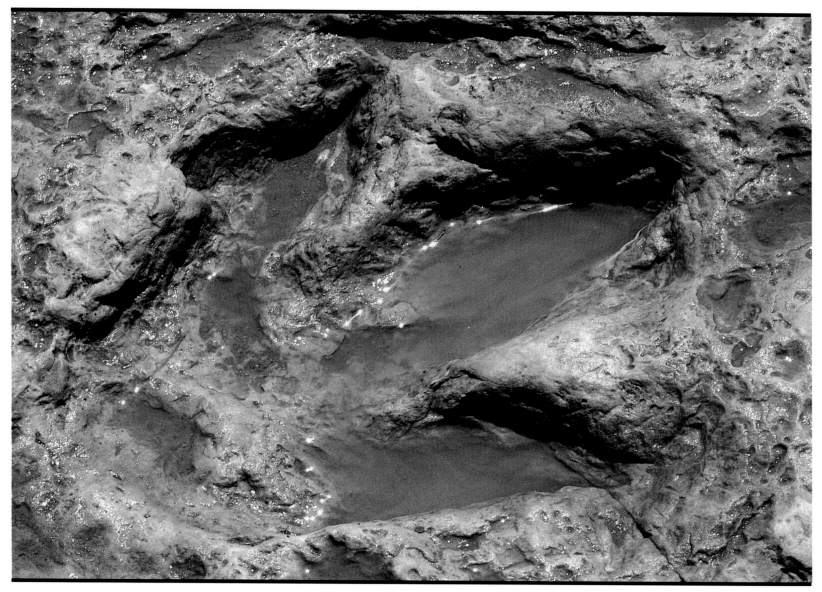

had feathers, as well as other birdlike characteristics; it has long been considered the link between birds and dinosaurs. Yet even this relationship has been called into question recently with the discovery of *Protoavis*, an even more birdlike dinosaur that lived millions of years before *Archaeopteryx*.

The similarities between dinosaurs, birds, and mammals don't end here. Like the American buffalo, the great horned *Triceratops* seems to have traveled in enormous herds, hundreds or thousands strong, probably in search of food. Stampeding across the vast plains of what is now the western United States, they must have made a spectacularly exciting sight—especially since the herds must have been pursued by *Tyrannosaurus* and other powerful meat-eaters also seeking their next meal.

These and other findings about dinosaur life—and the ever-present chance of discovering something even more exciting—should be enough to keep every dinosaur

© National Museum of Natural Sciences, Ottawa, Canada/painting by Eleanor Kish

© National Museum of Natural Sciences, Ottawa, Canada/painting by Eleanor Kish

Left: Dinosaurs, like this placid *Edmontosaurus*, were perfectly suited to their warm, food-rich environment. But they may have been unable to adapt to colder weather that killed off many types of plants.

Below: A likely extinction scenario: Following vast environmental changes, the plant-eating dinosaurs starved, providing a feast for these *Dromaeosaurs* and other predators. Soon enough, though, the bounty was gone, and the meat-eaters, too, marched into extinction.

hunter on earth busy. Yet nothing enthralls scientists and the public as much as a single question: Why did the great reptiles die out sixty-five million years ago?

Ever since we've known that the dinosaurs existed, we've been wondering how such powerful and diverse animals could have become extinct. Early theories included a plague of killer viruses, the rise of the mammals, and the dinosaurs' innate stupidity, but all these possibilities have long been discounted. More recently, the debate has shifted ground. Many paleontologists believe that the world changed in ways the dinosaurs simply couldn't adapt to. Intense volcanic activity and a gradual cooling of the earth's temperatures caused many plant species to die, followed by the plant-eating and then the meat-eating dinosaurs.

But other experts believe that the death of the dinosaurs was far more sudden and dramatic. This great extinction, they say, came as the result of an enormous explosion caused by the collision of an asteroid or comet with the earth. The cloud of dust raised by this impact obscured the sun and caused a months-long "winter," killing plants and animals, including the dinosaurs.

The controversy over the death of the dinosaurs shows no sign of abating, and debates about nesting dinosaurs, dinosaur-birds, and warm-blooded dinosaurs are also front-page material. Yet these and other arguments have succeeded in obscuring the main reason that we find the great reptiles so entrancing: the dinosaurs themselves.

In recent years, scientists have identified dozens of new types of dinosaurs, including many bizarre and wonderful creatures, to join the familiar *Triceratops* and *Tyrannosaurus*. From the chicken-sized *Compsognathus* to the 120-foot-(36-meter-) long *Seismosaurus*, from *Deinonychus* with its switchblade claw to the thick-headed *Pachycephalosaurus*, these and many other remarkable individuals form the foundation of our unending fascination with the great reptiles. Without the individuals that stalk across the pages that follow, there simply would be no dinosaur boom today.

Dinosaurs
A to Z

Key: The dinosaurs
in this section are
color coded as follows:

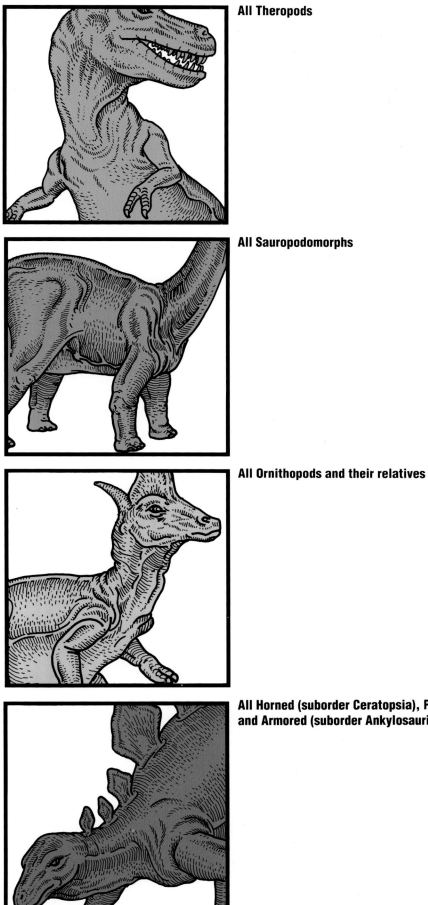

All Theropods

All Sauropodomorphs

All Ornithopods and their relatives

All Horned (suborder Ceratopsia), Plated (suborder Stegosauria), and Armored (suborder Ankylosauria) dinosaurs

Note: *The scale of the dinosaurs that appear in this section are approximate representations.*

Alamosaurus

("Alamo lizard"). A 70-foot (21-meter) sauropod that may have been the last of its kind to walk the earth. Oddly, while many dinosaurs, from the ceratopsians to the carnosaurs, produced their largest genus at the very end of the Cretaceous—just before the great extinction sixty-five million years ago—the sauropods didn't. The heyday of these enormous vegetarians came tens of millions of years earlier, during the Jurassic. Apparently common in what is now Texas (and named after the Alamo), *Alamosaurus* roamed as far north as Montana.

Acanthopolis

("Prickly scales"). An ankylosaur, it wore armor that would have made a medieval knight proud. (Actually, you could say that it was a combination of the knight and dragon in a single package.) *Acanthopolis* was 18 feet (5.5 meters) long, and boasted bony plates on its skin and spikes on its neck and back. Like all ankylosaurs, it probably didn't move very fast— but it didn't have to. It lived in England during the Cretaceous.

Allosaurus, Stegosaurus (here shown with two rows of plates), and *Diplodocus* probably never stood so close together by choice. But they did share the same tropical environment in the western United States during the Late Jurassic.

© Smithsonian Institution

Albertosaurus

("Alberta lizard"). In its northernmost haunts, *Alamosaurus* might have been hunted by this mid-sized carnosaur, which also roamed the Late Cretaceous grasslands of what is now Alberta, Canada (hence its name—although dozens of different dinosaurs could have been named after this remarkably fossil-rich province). Like its larger cousin, *Tyrannosaurus*, it had small, weak arms, but powerful jaws and legs.

Algoasaurus ("Algo lizard").

This little-known South African sauropod, which resembled the *Apatosaurus*, lived in the Early Cretaceous. The bones of this dinosaur, unearthed at the turn of the century, were among the first ever found in Africa. This exciting find helped convince scientists to journey to that continent in search of fossils. Within a decade, explorers were uncovering some of the greatest troves of dinosaur bones on earth.

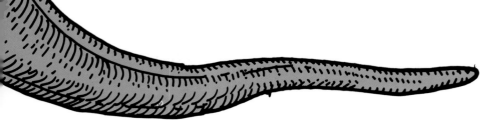

Allosaurus

("Different lizard"). One of the most famous of all dinosaurs, this meat-eater was also among the most widespread, ranging from North America to Australia and Africa. Its strong arms, sharp claws, and fearsome teeth gave it the look of an efficient hunter—but some scientists think that *Allosaurus* (and other large carnosaurs) may actually have survived by eating carrion.

Anatosaurus

("Duck lizard"). The "mummy" dinosaur was a Late Cretaceous duckbill whose skin and organs sometimes fossilized along with its skeleton. In the 1960s, the contents of one such mummy's stomach—pinecones and nuts that are found only in dry, highland areas—first convinced scientists that not all duckbills lived near water.

Anchisaurus

("Near lizard"). Prosauropods were comparatively primitive lizard-hipped dinosaurs that often barely resembled their more famous relatives, the sauropods. *Anchisaurus*, whose bones (found in Connecticut) were among the first-ever dug up in North America, was barely 7 feet (2 meters) in length, and may have weighed no more than 50 pounds (23 kilograms). It had blunt teeth, long hind legs, and shorter front legs whose hands were tipped with strong claws on the end of each thumb. This weird amalgam of characteristics make the experts unsure of whether *Anchisaurus* ate plants or meat—or possibly both.

Ankylosaurus

("Stiffened lizard"). At 30 feet (9 meters) or more, this was the largest of all ankylosaurs, and—as usual—one of the last; it died out in the extinction that saw the end of all dinosaurs. Occupying the same haunts as *Tyrannosaurus* and *Triceratops*, *Ankylosaurus* may have been one of the slowest dinosaurs of all time. But its spines, bony armor plates, and clublike tail must have told even the strongest predator that this was one dinosaur not to fool with.

Apatosaurus

("Deceptive lizard"). Think you've never heard of this sauropod? Sure you have—you just know it as *Brontosaurus*, the great "thunder lizard" of so many science fiction books, movies, and museum exhibits. In fact, you'll probably still see this 70-foot (21-meter) giant called by its more familiar name (though the name *Apatosaurus* was given first and used by scientists). By any name it was a massive, small-headed plant-eater that rumbled across the American West in Late Jurassic times.

Archaeopteryx ("Ancient feather"). This is one of the most famous, most beloved, and most controversial of all dinosaurs—and that's saying a lot, given the strong competition. First unearthed in Germany, it initially just looked like a well-preserved small coelurosaur. Then its discoverers looked again—and saw that this was a dinosaur with feathers.

Three-foot *Archaeopteryx*, which lived during the Late Jurassic, boasted many reptile characteristics: sharp teeth, a bony tail, and no large breastbone (which is found in all modern birds, but not in reptiles). Still, it had feathers, leading scientists on an ongoing quest to figure out its place in the dinosaur and bird world.

For many years, most scientists believed that *Archaeopteryx* was a missing link between birdlike dinosaurs, such as *Avimimus* (which may also have had feathers), and actual birds. But in recent years, others have begun to point out that true birds—complete with breastbones, far more powerful wings, and other advanced characteristics—showed up only a few million years after *Archaeopteryx*, far too quickly for the "ancient feather" to be their direct ancestor. Instead, *Archaeopteryx* may have been an evolutionary dead end—the dinosaur that didn't quite make it as a bird.

Despite these uncertainties, scientists agree that *Archaeopteryx* couldn't have been a very good flyer. Instead, it probably used its wings for balance as it pursued its prey, and perhaps for weak gliding.

Avimimus ("Bird mimic"). An interesting Late Cretaceous dinosaur, *Avimimus* shared a remarkable number of characteristics with modern birds, including large eyes, a large brain, long, three-toed feet, and lightweight bones. It may even have had feathers on its slender arms. Only 3 to 5 feet (92 centimeters to 1.6 meters) in length, agile *Avimimus* probably ran after the insects and small animals that made up its food.

Barapasaurus

("Big-leg lizard"). One of the most ancient of all sauropods, this 60-foot (18-meter) denizen of the Early Jurassic shared many characteristics with the even more ancient prosauropods. It had one feature that puzzles scientists: odd hollow chambers in its backbone. No one knows why, although these chambers must have had some use.

Barosaurus ("Heavy lizard").

The diplodocids, one family of sauropods, were among the longest dinosaurs, yet many were also very lightweight for their size. They must have presented an odd, gawky picture during the Late Jurassic, when they reached their greatest size and abundance. *Barosaurus* was 90 feet (27 meters) long; like the other diplodocids, it had a small, sloping head, weak teeth, and front legs that were far longer than those in back. It lived on the landmass that now constitutes North America and East Africa.

Daspletosaurus, a powerful carnosaur, stalked the plains of Alberta, Canada during the Late Cretaceous. Although it may have hunted *Triceratops* and other huge dinosaurs, here it seems to be considering making a meal of *Champsosaurus*, an ancestor of today's alligators.

Brachiosaurus

("Arm lizard"). Standing as much as 90 feet (27 meters) high and weighing 112 tons (110 metric tons), this may have been the most impressive of all sauropods—as well as one of the most unusual. Its front legs were extremely long (so its back sloped downward), and it also had a long neck and a high forehead, with its nostrils placed above the eyes. Its posture also made *Brachiosaurus* the tallest of all dinosaurs; its tiny head may have hovered a full 40 feet (12 meters) above the ground!

Camarasaurus

("Chambered lizard"). Yet another in a long line of Jurassic sauropods, this one was far more thickly and heavily built than many others. What makes *Camarasaurus* fascinating to scientists is not the creature itself, but a quirk of fate: Several skeletons of young *Camarasaurs* have been found. (The delicate, brittle bones of baby dinosaurs rarely fossilize in any recognizable form). *Camarasaurus* babies were remarkably stocky, with big heads, stumpy necks, and short tails.

In this evocative scene, a trio of *Camarasaurs* stalk across a field of mud toward a herd of *Camptosaurs*. Unwittingly, they left behind trackways, which scientists use today to learn about how the dinosaurs lived (following page).

Camptosaurus

("Bent lizard"). For years, paleontologists have debated whether many ornithopod dinosaurs walked on two legs or four. "Look," one argument went, "they have long hind legs and short front legs, just like any bipedal animal." "Okay," said the other side, "but take a closer look at the skeletal structure. A two-legged dinosaur wouldn't be built that way." So who's right? Examination of the *Camptosaurus* shows that both sides were correct: It had the powerful hind legs of a creature accustomed to striding around on two legs. But it also had tiny, hooflike claws on the end of each finger that made it clear that this dinosaur also walked on all fours.

Ceratosaurus

("Horned lizard"). In recent years, scientists have discovered more about the dinosaurs than previous experts could have ever imagined. But certain mysteries seem destined to remain unsolved forever. A case in point: What was the use of the small horn on the end of this Jurassic meat-eater's nose? It couldn't possibly have been used for hunting. Also, *Ceratosaurus'* teeth and claws would have been weapons enough. Perhaps males used the horn in sparring matches to impress the females or to achieve dominance in a herd. But we'll never know for sure.

© Doug Henderson

Coelophysis   ("Hollow body"). One of the earliest of all known dinosaurs, this slender, 10-foot (3-meter) hunter pursued and caught its prey, probably insects, lizards, and smaller dinosaurs. As is so often the case, we know so much about *Coelophysis* because of an ancient catastrophe. More than 200 million years ago, in what is now New Mexico, a violent sandstorm or other event killed dozens of *Coelophysis* of all sizes, whose fossilized skeletons lay undiscovered until 1947. Some of the larger skeletons had smaller ones inside them, which at first led scientists to think that they were examining unborn babies. Much more likely, the tiny skeletons were just unfortunate juvenile individuals that had recently been eaten by their adult relatives.

Compsognathus   ("Elegant jaw"). Quick, think of a dinosaur. What image comes to mind? You might visualize a giant *Tyrannosaurus* with slavering jaws or an *Apatosaurus* rumbling along on legs like pillars, but you certainly won't think of *Compsognathus*—one of the smallest dinosaurs ever known. Amazingly, this relative of *Coelurus* barely reached a length of 2 feet (61 centimeters), tail and all. It had slender, supple legs, which allowed it to hunt and catch fast-moving lizards and insects.

Deinocheirus ("Terrible hand"). Ready for a nightmare? Imagine a dinosaur so huge that each of its arms was more than 8 feet (2.5 meters) long. A creature whose hands were tipped in curved, dagger-sharp, 10-inch (26-centimeter) claws, each as lethal as a meat cleaver.

Does this sound unlikely? Well, believe it, because in 1965 scientists digging in Mongolia discovered the arms of a dinosaur—arms that fit this exact description. Nothing else of *Deinocheirus* has ever been found, so the experts remain unsure of exactly what this amazing Late Cretaceous dinosaur looked like. They do know that other dinosaurs must have treated it with respect.

Deinonychus

("Terrible claw"). How do dinosaur experts love *Deinonychus*? Let me count the ways.

First of all, it was one of the most fascinatingly designed of all dinosaurs. This 10-foot (3-meter) meat-eater was fearsomely equipped for hunting other dinosaurs: powerful hind legs, strong arms tipped with sharp claws, a stiffened tail that it used for balance, and—most impressive of all—a special 5-inch (13-centimeter), scythelike claw sprouting from each foot. With these weapons, scientists believe, a group of *Deinonychus* might have chased down even very large dinosaurs, then swung back on one leg and disemboweled the poor victim with their switchblades.

This advanced, active hunting technique gives rise to the second reason that *Deinonychus* is so beloved: No dinosaur has created more controversy, and scientists love controversy. Robert Bakker and others believe that *Deinonychus* must have been warm-blooded, that no cold-blooded dinosaur could possibly have evolved such an energetic hunting style. Many others disagree, and the debate shows no real sign of going away.

Dilophosaurus

("Two-ridged lizard"). An extremely early, primitive carnosaur, this relative of *Megalosaurus* grew to be about 20 feet (6 meters) in length. Like all of its kind, it walked mainly on two legs, and had sharp eyesight and knifelike teeth. It also had one unique attribute: a pair of fragile, bony ridges sitting like a thin crest atop its head. For a long time, scientists refused to believe that this delicate appurtenance came from *Dilophosaurus*, and even now they remain confused as to what its purpose was.

Diplodocus

("Double beam"). If you were a sauropod, you had no choice: You were blessed (or cursed) by certain physical attributes. You had a tiny head, a long neck, a massive body, four legs that resembled Grecian columns, and a seemingly endless, tapering tail. You also had a miniscule brain, and probably spent nearly all your time munching the tender leaves at the tops of trees only you could reach.

If you were *Diplodocus*, a Late Jurassic sauropod found in western North America, you had some of these typical features in abundance. For example, you were one of the longest of the sauropods—up to 90 feet (27 meters) in length—yet you weighed only about 12 tons (11 metric tons), far less than *Apatosaurus*, which weighed in at 30 tons (27 metric tons).

Take a good look at *Dilophosaurus's* remarkable crest. What could it have been used for? No one knows for sure, but it may have served as a prominent, colorful display, designed to attract a mate.

© Brian Regal/Melissa Turk & The Artist Network

Dravidosaurus ("Dravid lizard"). Perhaps the most unusual physical characteristic of this plated dinosaur was the spines on its tail, which featured odd bulges midway along their length. But what really distinguishes *Dravidosaurus* is when it lived: at the very end of the Late Cretaceous, tens of millions of years after *Stegosaurus* and most others. *Dravidosaurus* was the last stegosaur, the one that might have witnessed the end of the dinosaurs' world.

Dromaeosaurus ("Swift lizard"). A pint-sized version of *Deinonychus*, complete with a large brain, strong arms, and a curved claw on each foot. Though only 6 feet (2 meters) long, it probably hunted and killed much bigger dinosaurs, as well as lizards and other smaller prey. Like its larger relative, *Dromaeosaurus* has aroused controversy, with many scientists positive that a sluggish, cold-blooded dinosaur simply could not have managed this fierce little dinosaur's active hunting technique.

Another inhabitant of the marvelously rich Alberta forests and plains, *Dromiceiomimus* may have used its huge eyes to hunt at dawn and dusk, when other dinosaurs were inactive.

Dromiceiomimus

("Emu mimic"). This mid-sized ornithomimid (reaching a length of about 11 feet [3.5 meters]) had all of that family's interesting quirks and characteristics. *Dromiceiomimus* had a large brain (bigger than an ostrich's), slim but powerful legs, and huge eyes that would have enabled it to remain active at dusk. It lived in the Late Cretaceous in what is now Alberta, Canada—a region that must have been literally crawling with dinosaurs.

Dryptosaurus ("Wounding lizard").

Here lies a perfect illustration of how dinosaur hunters sometimes let their fantasies run away with them. When famed paleontologist Edward Drinker Cope unearthed this Late Cretaceous carnosaur, he decided (from sparse fossil evidence) that it used its strong hind legs to leap like a kangaroo onto its prey. Today, scientists won't go so far, and are eagerly awaiting more substantial fossil finds before hazarding any guesses as to *Dryptosaurus'* life and habits.

Edmontosaurus ("Edmonton lizard"). One of those duckbills not fortunate enough to have a bizarre crest or other protuberance, this Late Cretaceous genus made up for it with several other distinctive characteristics: great size (43 feet [13 meters]), an enormous number of teeth (perhaps a thousand), and, most endearingly, a pair of loose skin flaps on its head that it might have been able to inflate.

Elaphorosaurus ("Lightweight lizard"). Every once in a while, scientists make a discovery that is particularly special to them, and this ostrich dinosaur is one of them. There is nothing particularly distinctive about *Elaphorosaurus*—except that it lived in the Late Jurassic, seventy million years before all other known ornithomimids. Clumsier than its later relatives, probably unable to run nearly as fast, it was still a fleet-footed and agile predator.

Euoplocephalus

("Well-armored head"). A common North American ankylosaur, *Euoplocephalus* was also a good demonstration of what made those walking tanks so remarkable. Euoplocephalus wore a thick coat of armor that included spines, ridges, bony plates, and probably chunks of bone planted just beneath the skin. But perhaps most impressive was its tail: The last few bones were fused into a solid block tipped with a large club. Even *Tyrannosaurus* would have hesitated before attacking a dinosaur equipped with such powerful defenses.

Fabrosaurus

("Fabre's lizard"). This tiny, primitive ornithischian dinosaur was part of a group that may have developed into all other bird-hipped dinosaurs. Found only in a single region of Southern Africa, it was a lightly-built, 3-foot (92-centimeter) plant-eater that ran on its hind legs. Like a herbivorous dinosaur, it must have lost teeth frequently while chewing on tough leaves and seeds. But new teeth would grow in to replace those that fell out.

From dry grasslands and forested hills to humid swamps, the wonderfully diverse dinosaurs (including these *Edmontosaurs*) occupied every terrain on earth.

Gallimimus ("Rooster mimic"). At 13 feet (4 meters), this dinosaur was one of the biggest of all ornithomimids, those birdlike dinosaurs that reached their greatest variety in the Late Cretaceous. With their long, slender legs, skinny necks, and light-boned heads equipped with toothless beaks, *Gallimimus* and the other bird mimics really did resemble such familiar birds as ostriches. They may also have behaved very similarly, striding warily across the plains and scanning the horizon with a sharp eye out for approaching predators.

Garudimimus ("Garuda mimic"). This recently described dinosaur was clearly related to the ostrich dinosaurs, but it differed in many ways. It had, for example, a far more rounded beak and a crest on top of its head. Unlike those other bird mimics, however, *Garudimimus* had very large eyes.

Hadrosaurus ("Large lizard"). The *Hadrosaurus* is the namesake for the hadrosaurs, that huge group of duck-billed dinosaurs, abundant in Late Cretaceous times. All were ornithopods that apparently walked easily either on their hind legs or on all fours. They had broad skulls and powerful jaws designed to grind tough vegetation, and many boasted mysterious but wonderfully varied crests. *Hadrosaurus*, unearthed in Alberta, Canada in 1858, was one of the first dinosaurs to be discovered in North America.

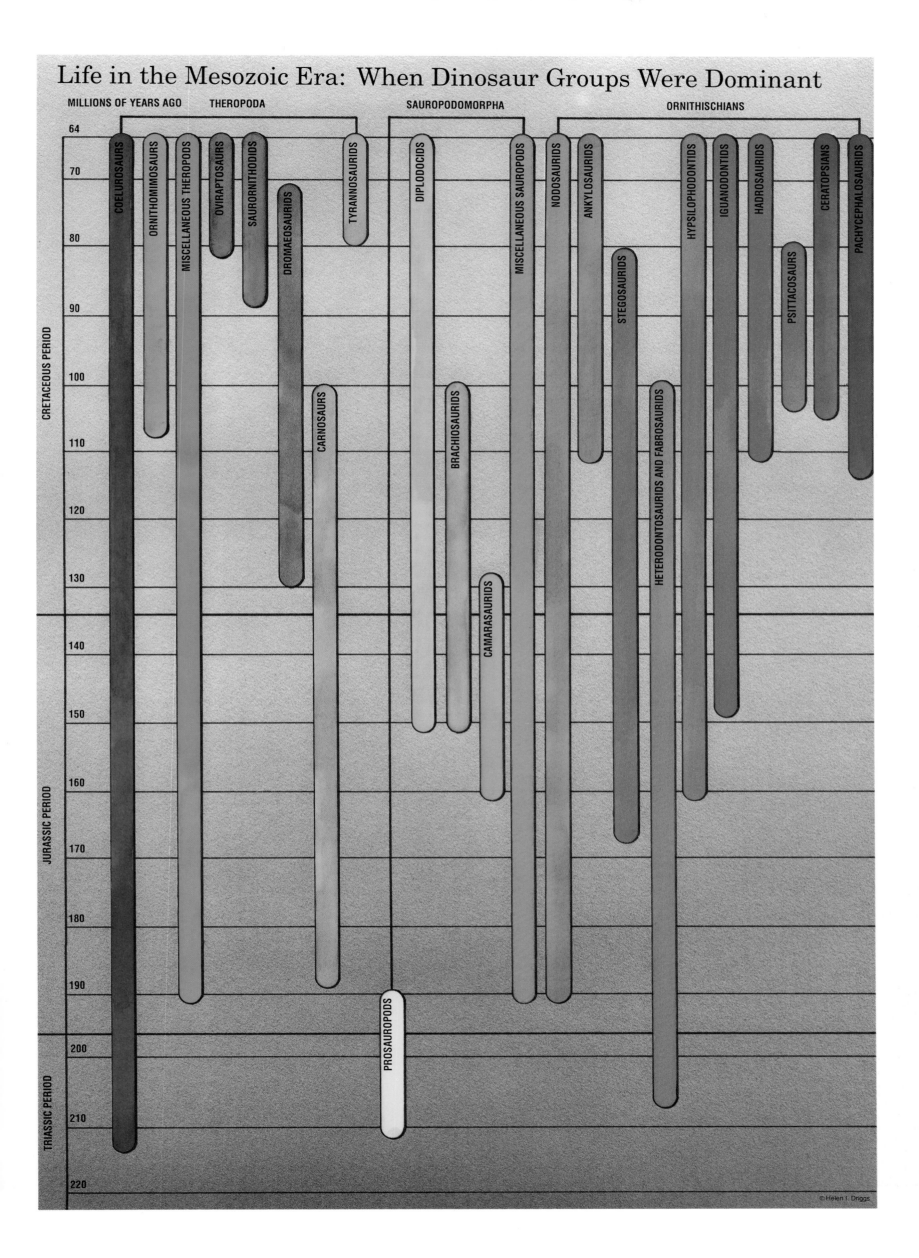

Life in the Mesozoic Era: When Dinosaur Groups Were Dominant

Herrerasaurus

("Herrera lizard"). This early, rather primitive lizard-hipped dinosaur was clearly a formidable predator. One of the few dinosaurs whose fossils have been found in South America, this Late Triassic hunter grew to about 10 feet (3 meters), yet weighed only about 200 pounds (75 kilograms). It boasted sharp, curving teeth, long, powerful arms, and individual bones that resembled both those of prosauropods and those of theropods. No one knows yet exactly who *Herrerasaurus'* closest relatives were.

Heterodontosaurus

("Different-toothed lizard"). This was one of the earliest—and most unusual—ornithopods. Roaming Late Triassic or Early Jurassic South Africa, this 4-foot (1.2-meter) dinosaur had three different types of teeth: sharp incisors in front, large molars in the cheek, and pairs of odd, curving tusks growing beside the incisors. No one knows what these tusks may have been used for—or even exactly what *Heterodontosaurus* ate with its strange teeth.

© Doug Henderson

With their large size and ponderous bulk, *Iguanodons* may have sought safety in small herds or family groups. Even so, they likely were frequent prey of local meat-eaters.

Homalocephale ("Even head").

A mid-sized pachycephalosaur, or bonehead dinosaur, found in Mongolia—that hotbed of odd and fascinating fossils. It featured a particularly flat, rough skull, covered—as in many boneheads—with bumps and knobs of bone. But the most interesting discovery about *Homalocephale* has nothing to do with its head, and everything to do with its hips: Some scientists believe that the shape of this dinosaur's hip bones indicates that it didn't lay eggs, but gave birth to live young. By the way, this isn't so astounding. Today, several snake species, including the common North American garter snake, hold the eggs internally until they are ready to hatch, and then give birth to active young, which are immediately ready to strike off on their own. This is very different from the live births seen in warm-blooded birds and mammals, in which the babies are helpless and must be taken care of for days to years.

No one knows if *Hypacrosaurus* was really camouflage green. But there is little doubt that the dinosaurs were far more colorful than early artists (and scientists) thought. This duckbill's leafy environment may well have encouraged the development of green skin.

Hypacrosaurus ("High-ridged lizard"). No dinosaurs were odder looking or more ungainly than the duckbills, with their thick legs, spatula-like mouths, and peculiar crests. *Hypacrosaurus* was one of the largest, about 30 feet (9 meters) in length; its crest formed a high bump atop its skull, leading to a sharp spike that pointed down its back. Even today, scientists argue over the possible purposes of *Hypacrosaurus'* (and other duckbills') crests.

Hypselosaurus

("High lizard"). While the heyday
of the sauropods was the Jurassic period (which saw such
familiar examples as *Apatosaurus*, *Diplodocus*, and
Brachiosaurus), many of the great beasts did survive through
the Cretaceous. This mid-sized sauropod—about 40 feet (12
meters) long—was a typical example.

Less typical, however, was the discovery of large
numbers of eggs found near the bones of *Hypselosaurus* in
France. The eggs, the only ones ever identified as having been
laid by a sauropod, were about 12 inches (35 centemeters)
long—big for dinosaur eggs, but very small for the size of the
parent. The eggs were thick-shelled and bumpy.

Hypsilophodon

("High-ridged tooth"). It wasn't very
long ago that scientists thought that all
dinosaurs were plodding, slow-moving
creatures—but they don't think so
anymore, and speedsters like this Early
Cretaceous ornithopod are part of the
reason why. With its supple feet, long
shins, powerful thighs, and stiffened tail for
balance, *Hypsilophodon* was clearly a sprinter, much like an
antelope today. It must have nipped vegetation with its bony
beak and chewed with its ridged cheek teeth which were perfectly
adapted for pulverizing even the toughest leaves and branches.

Iguanodon ("Iguana tooth").
This thickset Early Cretaceous ornithopod was an abundant ancestor of the widespread duckbills that dominated the Late Cretaceous. Thirty feet (9 meters) long, with a massive head and heavy tail, it was not the most graceful of dinosaurs. Perhaps its most unusual feature was a sharp spike replacing the thumb on each hand—a spike that might have been used as a weapon.

Iguanodon was also one of the earliest dinosaurs to be discovered and identified as a huge, extinct reptile. Gideon and Mary Ann Mantell discovered fossils of this genus in England in 1822. One of the most entertaining sidelights of *Iguanodon*'s recent history is the early reconstruction of this dinosaur, which showed it as a lumbering, bulky lizard with a tiny horn on its nose. (The horn, of course, was *Iguanodon*'s thumb spike, but only one had turned up when the reconstruction was made.)

Ingenia ("Genius"). Yet another recently discovered oddball Mongolian dinosaur, further proof that this Chinese desert must still contain untold fascinating finds. *Ingenia*, related to the ostrich dinosaurs, was a 6-foot (1.8-meter) meat-eater with powerful hind legs, short, thick fingers, and a toothless jaw ending in a powerful beak. It probably ate eggs, although it might also have hunted or scavenged meat or bones.

Lambeosaurus ("Lambe's lizard"). Another odd duckbill, and at 50 feet (15 meters) in length, one of the biggest and most massive of all time. *Lambeosaurus* had a large, square crest with a sharp spike sticking out from the back of the crest, as if it were wearing a huge mitten on its head. Its air passages ran through the crest, for reasons that remain unclear to this day.

Maiasaura ("Good-mother lizard"). In 1979, paleontologists John Horner and Robert Makela made a dinosaur discovery that turned the paleontology field upside down. In a barren region of Montana, they unearthed a slew of skeletons of a previously unknown duckbill, a 30-foot (9-meter) creature that physically wasn't very different from many other species. What was different—and exciting—was the discovery of fossilized mud nests, enough of them to prove for the first time that at least one type of dinosaur lived and bred in colonies.

But what astounded the two scientists was that the skeletons included some of tiny babies, others of half-grown individuals, and still others of adults. So it became clear that—unlike any other reptile known—*Maiasaura* must have cared for its babies for months, even years, protecting them and bringing them food, much as birds do today.

Mamenchisaurus   ("Mamenchin lizard"). More or less, every sauropod looked alike. But only more or less. This remarkable Late Jurassic individual, whose bones were found in southern China, stands out for one simple feature: its neck. The beast itself was about 70 feet (21 meters) long—and a full half the length was made up by its neck. This 35-foot (11-meter) extravaganza contained nineteen vertebrae, more than any other dinosaur. Rods of bone running alongside the vertebrae provided needed strength and stability to a neck that must have been a remarkable sight.

Massospondylus   ("Massive vertebrae"). At first glance, many of the Late Triassic prosauropods looked like small, primitive ancestors of the huge sauropods that strode across the Late Jurassic. For example, prosauropods had long necks and tapering tails, much like their more famous relatives.

But, as this 13-foot (4-meter) individual shows, prosauropods and sauropods had some distinctive differences. *Massospondylus* had very strong and flexible hind legs, and its front legs ended in grasping hands, including a thumb equipped with a curving claw. These features make it likely that *Massospondylus*, like other prosauropods but unlike the sauropods, may have spent some time walking on its hind legs.

Maiasaurs may have been one of the most common dinosaurs along the eastern front of the Rocky Mountains during the Cretaceous. We know that because so many thousands of them were killed by an enormous ashfall eighty million years ago.

© Doug Henderson

Megalosaurus   ("Huge lizard"). All right, all right, I know what you're thinking: "All he's telling us about are undignified duckbills, plodding prosauropods, and obscure ornithopods. Where are all the fun dinosaurs? Where are the horrifying predators with the blood dripping from their fangs? That's what we're reading this book for."

Say hello to *Megalosaurus*, the first dinosaur ever to be named and one of the best-designed predators in the history of the earth. Smaller than its more familiar cousins *Allosaurus* and *Tyrannosaurus*, *Megalosaurus* may have been faster on its feet and more agile than those great meat-eaters. With strong, curving claws on its feet and hands, and long, serrated teeth, it would have been a threat to any dinosaur that crossed its path.

Melanorosaurus ("Black-mountain lizard," also known as *Euskelosaurus*). Until fairly recently, experts thought that the great sauropods were direct descendants of prosauropods—and this 40-foot (12-meter) plodder was powerful evidence for that theory. Huge, heavy, and possessing four legs good only for walking (unlike other prosauropods, which had arms and hands), Late Triassic *Melanorosaurus* did, in fact, closely resemble the sauropods.

But in paleontology (to paraphrase Yogi Berra), you don't know *nothin'*. Today, many scientists think that prosauropods and sauropods were just different branches on the same family tree, with no direct relationship.

Mussasaurus ("Mouse lizard"). Okay, had your fill of giant dinosaurs? Well, take a look at something completely different: *Mussasaurus*, the world's smallest dinosaur.

Actually, we don't know for sure if this prosauropod was the smallest dinosaur—but we do know that its babies (and probably its eggs) were incredibly tiny. A fossilized egg that scientists think was laid by a *Mussasaurus* measured about an inch (3 centimeters) in length. Almost as amazing, babies found in a nest were no longer than 8 inches (24 centimeters). That's about as big as a robin.

Muttaburrasaurus ("Muttaburra lizard"). As well as having one of the most endearing of all dinosaur names, this Late Cretaceous relative of *Iguanodon* is one of the only dinosaurs ever found in Australia. Experts think that many more dinosaur remains will eventually be found in Australia, once enough scientists brave its harsh deserts in the search for fossils.

Nanotyrannus ("Pygmy tyrant"). One of the things that makes the world of dinosaurs so fascinating and enjoyable to follow is that—despite the fact that the great reptiles have been extinct for sixty-five million years—nothing in paleontology stays the same for very long.

Back in 1942, dinosaur hunters in Montana brought a load of fossils to the Cleveland Museum of Natural History in Ohio. Among these fossils was the skull of what they thought was an *Albertosaurus*, a very common Late Cretaceous carnosaur. The museum already had good examples of *Albertosaurus*, so the skull was labeled and filed away, where it lay untouched for many years.

Then, in 1988, a group of paleontologists headed by Robert Bakker challenged the identification. By examining the skull closely, they found that it actually shared many characteristics with *Tyrannosaurus*, although it weighed only one-tenth as much.

Yet the fully fused bones showed that the skull must have belonged to a previously unknown adult dinosaur, and not a baby tyrannosaur.

Nanotyrannus was, scientists think, an exact, although miniaturized, replica of its famous giant cousin. Reaching a length of about 17 feet (5.3 meters), and weighing in at about 1000 pounds (455 kilograms), it was equipped with a large brain, relatively weak arms and hands, and a long, narrow muzzle filled with sharp, curving, serrated teeth. In other words, this pygmy tyrant must have been an agile, powerful hunter.

Noasaurus ("Northwest Argentina lizard"). A South American relative of *Deinonychus*, this Late Cretaceous theropod was smaller than its fearsome relative. But, it too, featured a slashing switchblade claw, with which it may have attacked far larger dinosaurs. If, as many scientists believed, coelurosaurs (including *Noasaurus*) often hunted in packs, they may have been the most feared dinosaur predators of all.

Opisthocoelicauda   ("Backward hollow tail"). This unusual Late Cretaceous sauropod illustrates what makes paleontology both a rewarding and a frustrating profession. When a nearly complete skeleton of this 40-foot (12-meter) dinosaur was discovered in the Gobi Desert in Mongolia, scientists soon found that it had an odd set of tail bones that may have allowed it to prop itself up on its hind legs. But the fossil record giveth and taketh away: This skeleton was missing a head and neck, and no others have ever been found, so the experts have never been able to study *Opisthocoelicauda* thoroughly enough.

Ornitholestes   ("Bird robber"). Another one of those swift, lightweight hunters that don't fit in with the theory that dinosaurs were heavy-footed creatures. No more than 7 feet (2.2 meters) long, with a slender neck, grasping hands, and powerful legs, *Ornitholestes* got its name from its supposed ability to catch birds. More likely, it pursued and grabbed lizards and small mammals.

Ornithomimus

("Bird mimic"). The namesake of the ornithomimids or ostrich dinosaurs, it came from a large group of remarkable dinosaurs that closely resembled ostriches, emus, and other large, flightless birds in both shape and behavior. *Ornithomimus* was about 12 feet (4 meters) long, had extremely thin and supple legs, skinny arms, a very slender neck, and a small head equipped with a bony beak and large eyes. *Ornithomimus* and its relatives could run fast—perhaps even faster than a galloping horse.

Orodromeus

("Mountain runner"). One of the latest of the seemingly unending slew of fascinating dinosaur discoveries made by Jack Horner in Montana, this member of the hypsilophodontid family (which also contains *Dryosaurus* and other antelope-like dinosaurs) was itself cause for celebration.

But what made this 1987 find even more exciting was that it came with a clutch of nineteen unhatched eggs, many of which contained fossilized skeletons of the enclosed embryos. Using CT scans (high-powered x-rays), Horner and his coworkers were able to study the embryos closely, and identify them as belonging to a newly created genus and species: *Orodromeus makelai*. It reached a length of about 8 feet (2.5 meters), they believe, and was (like most of its family) among the fastest-moving of all dinosaurs.

Ouranosaurus ("Brave lizard").
Scientists think this Early Cretaceous
relative of *Iguanodon* had one unusual
characteristic: a large skin "sail" on its back.
Of course, this sail hasn't survived the
millennia, but spines standing erect from
the dinosaur's backbone almost certainly evolved to
support such a flap of skin. The sail might have been
used as a "heat exchanger": That is, when the dinosaur
was cold, turning the sail to the sun would have enabled
it to absorb extra rays. On the other hand, on a hot day,
Ouranosaurus could have sought shade, then radiated
heat more rapidly through the skin flap.

Oviraptor   ("Egg robber").
Although related to the ostrich dinosaurs,
this 6-foot (1.85-meter) meat-eater
boasted several fascinating features
of its own. Like those slender
reptiles, it was built for speed and hunting, with
strong legs, grasping hands, and a toothless jaw
ending in a beak. But *Oviraptor* had
remarkably powerful jaws for a dinosaur its
size; its beak would easily have chewed up bones, as
well as the eggs that it probably also ate.

Pachycephalosaurus

("Thick-headed lizard"). For unclear reasons, the Late Cretaceous was the glory period for bizarre dinosaurs—and few were odder than the *Pachycephalosaurs* or bonehead dinosaurs. These two-legged plant-eaters had bodies that resembled the duckbills, but skulls that looked like nothing else on earth. Nearly every bonehead had a massively thick, domed skull; *Pachycephalosaurus'* was 10 inches (25 centimeters) thick!

What was the purpose of such thick skulls? We may never know for sure, but some experts believe that male boneheads might have fought for dominance in the herd by banging their heads together, much as bighorn sheep do today.

Pachycephalosaurus itself was the biggest bonehead, with the thickest skull. It grew to be about 15 feet (5 meters) in length, and lived, like so many other Late Cretaceous dinosaurs, in western North America.

Pachyrhinosaurus

("Thick-nosed lizard"). When is a horned dinosaur not a horned dinosaur? When it's *Pachyrhinosaurus*, a relative of the familiar *Triceratops* that came equipped with no horns at all. Instead, it had a mass of bone between its eyes that couldn't have provided a very effective weapon. Its chief protection must have been its large size (up to 20 feet [6.2 meters]) and thick, tough skin.

Panoplosaurus

Panoplosaurus ("Fully-armored lizard"). Another dinosaur that must have relied on size and body armor was the *Panoplosaurus*, one of the last of all ankylosaurs. Its arched skull was protected by thick bone, and nearly impregnable bony plates lined its back. For a roving predator, attempting to kill *Panoplosaurus* must have been about as easy as opening a can of tuna without an opener.

Parasaurolophus

Parasaurolophus ("Like *Saurolophus*"). Among the duckbills—a group of dinosaurs well-known for their bizarre appearance—*Parasaurolophus* somehow managed to be even weirder than most of the rest. Its body was a typical duckbill's: thickset, with strong hind legs, fleshy arms, and a flat, ducklike mouth. But atop its skull stood an amazing hollow horn up to 6 feet (1.8 meters) long. And that's not all: The dinosaur's breathing passages ran from its nostrils up one side of the horn, down the other, and out into the creature's mouth.

Why? Good question—one that scientists still aren't sure they have the answer to. But some think that the hollow horn (found, in various shapes, in many duckbills) might have functioned as an echo chamber, allowing the dinosaur to make loud honking sounds. These might have been used in sexual display, as a threat mechanism, or merely to keep in touch with other members of a herd.

Pentaceratops

("Five-horned face"). Forget *Pachyrhinosaurus*—this is a *real* horned dinosaur. With one spike on its nose, two long ones on its forehead, and a small one on each cheek, this ornate ceratopsian also featured an enormous neck frill. It roamed what is now the southwestern United States during the Late Cretaceous, and may have run in vast herds as the *Triceratops* did.

Pinacosaurus

("Board lizard"). There is nothing very special about this 18-foot (5.5-meter) Late Cretaceous ankylosaur. Like many of its relatives, it had bony plates protecting its skull, thick skin, and teeth designed for grinding up vegetation.

Nothing special—except it had a pair of extra holes near its nostrils. Holes that no scientist has been able to figure out the purpose of. Holes that prove once again that there is still a lot we don't know about the dinosaurs.

Plateosaurus

("Flat lizard"). Without a doubt the best-known of all prosauropods, those mysterious early relatives of the great Jurassic sauropods. *Plateosaurus* is well known for one very good reason: It was apparently very common, and many of its skeletons have survived in good condition. So we know that it reached a length of about 25 feet (7.6 meters), that it had a long but rather thick neck, and that it probably spent most of its time walking on all fours. However, it could rear up on its hind legs if it wanted to reach some succulent vegetation.

Prosaurolophus ("Before *Saurolophus*"). Sometimes it seems that scientists allow their hopes to carry them away. Hence this Late Cretaceous duckbill's name. Yes, it bore marked similarities to *Saurolophus*, which lived several million years later. Yes, it may well have been that duckbill's direct ancestor (which would make it very special, as scientists have had a terrible time tracing any sort of accurate dinosaur family tree). But, given the vagaries of the fossil record, and the sixty-five million years that have passed since the last one disappeared, who's to know for sure?

Protoavis ("First bird"). Scientists have known for many years that dinosaurs and birds are closely related. Perhaps the most telling evidence of all has been the 150-million-year-old *Archaeopteryx*, that small dinosaur with a feathered tail and arms whose nineteenth-century discovery in Germany shook the scientific world. For many years, *Archaeopteryx* has been considered the likely ancestor of modern birds.

But some scientists have long doubted that birds could have evolved directly from *Archaeopteryx*, for one good reason: Such advanced birds as herons and gulls began to appear just a few million years after *Archaeopteryx's* heyday, and evolution simply doesn't work that fast.

In 1986, a Texas paleontologist named Sankar Chatterjee made a stunning announcement. He had found, he said, a fossil skeleton that contained far more bird-like qualities than did *Archaeopteryx*—but also shared many characteristics with the dinosaurs. For example, *Protoavis* (as he named it) had strong hind legs, a bony tail, and a dinosaur-like pelvis. But the skeleton also contained a bird's large eye sockets, hollow bones, a large wishbone, and a breastbone featuring a keel, used by birds to anchor flight muscles.

Perhaps most exciting of all, however, was *Protoavis'* age. It lived at the dawn of the late Triassic period, 225 million years ago. This places it seventy-five million years before the appearance of *Archaeopteryx*, and even further before the first advanced bird. Therefore, *Protoavis* may in fact be the missing link we've been seeking for decades: the world's first bird.

Protoceratops ("First horned face"). Only 6 feet

(1.8 meters) long, this earliest known horned dinosaur was dwarfed by such later arrivals as *Triceratops*. It had no horns, but its curving beak, large neck frill, and other features left no doubt that it was a ceratopsian. Probably the most interesting thing about *Protoceratops* was discovered by famed explorer Roy Chapman Andrews during a 1922 expedition to Mongolia. Here Andrews came upon undisturbed nests containing eggs and skeletons of newly hatched young that he identified as *Protoceratops*. They must have died during a sandstorm or other ancient calamity.

Psittacosaurus ("Parrot lizard").

An odd horned dinosaur that, aside from its large, beaked head, resembled an ornithopod more than a ceratopsian—although one type did have a tiny (and seemingly useless) horn on its nose. No more than 6 feet (1.8 meters) in length, *Psittacosaurus* was apparently comfortable both on all fours and on two legs. Its rather small front legs ended in hands that the dinosaur might have used to pull vegetation from bushes and trees.

Saltasaurus ("Salta lizard"). A very strange Late Cretaceous sauropod, first described in 1980. Only 40 feet (12 meters) long, it had hundreds of bone plates lining the skin of its back. Ranging from a fraction of an inch to 4 inches (13 centimeters) in length, these plates must have provided protection against the predators that stalked its South American range.

Saurolophus ("Ridged lizard"). Every duckbill, it sometimes seems, had at least one odd characteristic. Thirty-foot (9-meter) *Saurolophus* had a strange sloping skull that scientists think was covered with flaps of skin. It may have been able to inflate these flaps into balloons, perhaps to impress members of the opposite sex.

Saurornithoides ("Birdlike lizard").

Even if most everyone loves the dinosaurs, few people think of them as having much in the way of intelligence. Yet here was a dinosaur with a brain proportionately far larger than most other reptiles'. With its huge eyes designed for accurate long-distance sighting, light frame, and sharp claws and teeth, *Saurornithoides* must have been a formidable foe. Its superb vision may have allowed it to hunt in near-darkness, when most other dinosaurs were already bedded down for the night. Some paleontologists believe that this was the same dinosaur as the *Stenonychosaurus*.

Saurornitholestes

("Lizard-bird robber"). Another in a long list of "terrible claw" dinosaurs—those remarkably intelligent and fierce Late Cretaceous descendants of *Deinonychus*. *Saurornitholestes* was far smaller, only about 6 feet (1.8 meters) in length, but it made up in weaponry what it sacrificed in size. Along with the switchblade claws found throughout the family, it boasted sharp, serrated teeth, and strong, grasping hands that ended in hook-shaped claws—perfect for grabbing and holding onto far larger prey.

Scelidosaurus

("Limb lizard"). This low-slung dinosaur, which moved slowly through Early Jurassic Europe, was one of the most primitive of all armored dinosaurs. Lacking the solid armor, large bony plates, spikes, and clubs that protected later ankylosaurs and stegosaurs, it made do with rows of small chunks of bone imbedded in its skin. Even this protection must have prevented all but the most powerful predators from attacking *Scelidosaurus*.

Scutellosaurus   ("Little-shield lizard").

As *Saltasaurus* showed earlier, not only the armored dinosaurs came equipped with protection. This Early Jurassic ornithopod was only 4 feet (1.2 meters) long, so it couldn't have stood up to local meat-eaters in search of a meal. But *Scutellosaurus*, like *Scelidosaurus*, harbored hundreds of small, bony studs along its back. Presumably, a mid-sized predator might break a tooth on this thick skin, allowing *Scutellosaurus* to escape.

© Doug Henderson

Segisaurus ("Segi lizard"). An odd, little-known Jurassic dinosaur that deserves mention because it doesn't seem closely related to any other dinosaur. Unfortunately (but not unusually), all that is known about it comes from some incomplete skeletons found in Arizona. From what's been studied, however, *Segisaurus* is thought to be related to the coelurosaurs, and perhaps most similar to *Procompsognathus*, with which it shares long, slender hind legs. Unlike the lightweight coelurosaurs, however, *Segisaurus* had solid bones—so it probably wasn't as agile and didn't move as fast as those fleet hunters.

Segnosaurus ("Slow lizard"). Despite more than a century of intensive searching, paleontologists still frequently come upon fossils of dinosaurs they've never seen before. Many of these, for some reason, have been found in Mongolia, a barren, harsh landscape that remains one of the richest fossil sites on earth. Beginning in the late 1970s, scientists began to uncover the remains of a group of very odd Late Cretaceous saurischians—lizard-hipped dinosaurs so unlike any others that they were soon placed in their own infraorder: segnosauria, or "slow lizards."

What made *Segnosaurus* and its relatives so unusual? First, they had many features seen previously only in bird-hipped dinosaurs. For example, *Segnosarus'* hip bones closely resembled those of ornithischians, as did its toothless beak. Yet it also had rows of sharp teeth—clearly designed for meat-eating—in the back of its jaw.

Experts think that this 30-foot (9-meter) maverick may have spent much of its time in the water, chasing and catching fish.

Previous page: Watch out for stampeding sauropods! Throughout the age of the dinosaurs, environmental cataclysms killed vast numbers of the great reptiles—and left fossils for us to discover millions of years later.

Seismosaurus ("Earthshaker lizard"). A little later you'll read about *Supersaurus* and *Ultrasaurus*, two enthusiastically named sauropods that—at the time of their discoveries in the 1970s—were the longest dinosaurs ever known. *Seismosaurus* comes first alphabetically, which is only appropriate, for right now this Jurassic sauropod is the biggest dinosaur ever.

Unearthed in 1986 in New Mexico, its fossils indicate that *Seismosaurus* may have reached the unbelievable length of 120 feet (36 meters), and a weight of 100 tons (99 metric tons). To put this in perspective, a large elephant may weigh about 8 to 10 tons (7.2 to 9 metric tons)—and elephants are the heaviest animals living on land today.

Of course, *Seismosaurus* may only hold its crown for a brief time. Paleontologist David Gillette, who excavated it, believes that other, larger sauropods may soon be unearthed from the rich fossil bed.

Shantungosaurus

("Shantung lizard"). The largest duckbill yet found, this Chinese plant-eater may have been nearly 50 feet (15 meters) in length—as big as a *Tyrannosaurus*. In classic duckbill fashion, it was heavyset, with thick, strong legs and short, fleshy arms. But, unlike its more outlandish relatives, it apparently had no crest.

Spinosaurus

("Spiny lizard"). Each type of dinosaur usually boasted at least one feature that truly distinguished it from all others. Horned dinosaurs had sharp spikes and expansive neck frills; duckbills had odd, hollow crests; armored dinosaurs had impregnable skin and clublike tails. But in almost every group there is at least one (and usually many more) that doesn't fit the mold. Take a look at *Spinosaurus*, a Late Cretaceous combination of a carnosaur and a sailboat.

Forty feet (12 meters) long, with teeth like knives, *Spinosaurus* was clearly a relative of *Tyrannosaurus* and other Late Cretaceous meat-eaters. But fossil finds have proven that it had enormous spines sticking up from its backbone. These spines—some a full 6 feet (1.8 meters) long—must have supported a massive sail of skin that ran along the reptile's back. This sail, scientists believe, probably functioned as a heat exchanger, gathering the sun's rays in the cool morning and evening, allowing *Spinosaurus* to vent heat during the hotter parts of the day.

Staurikosaurus   ("Cross lizard").

Another strange, primitive Late Triassic dinosaur, which roamed what is now Brazil. Only about 6 feet (1.8 meters) tall, lightly built, with sharp teeth, a large head, and a very long tail, *Staurikosaurus* resembled both early prosauropods (which ate plants) and theropods (which ate meat). Exactly what group it fell into will not be decided until paleontologists find more fossils of either *Staurikosaurus* itself or of its close relatives.

Stegosaurus

("Plated lizard"). One of the best-known and most-beloved of all dinosaurs, this 30-foot (9-meter) armored stegosaur was also the biggest of its kind. It had a tiny head (with a brain the size of a walnut), short front legs, a huge, heavy body, and a thick, tapering tail. But *Stegosaurus*' most famous features were the large plates that ran in a row down its back, and the vicious spikes that tipped its tail.

Look in nearly any dinosaur book, and you'll see *Stegosaurus* illustrated as having *two* rows of alternating plates on its back. In 1986, however, sculptor Stephen Czerkas built a scientifically accurate model of the dinosaur showing that the *Stegosaurus*' bone and muscle structure allowed it only a single row of plates. Now most experts agree that this was the real *Stegosaurus*, and that the dinosaur used the plates less as armor than as heat exchangers, much like *Spinosaurus*'s sail.

What's wrong with this picture? If you noticed that the *Stegosaurus* had two rows of plates on its back, and knew that scientists now agree that the huge dinosaur had only one row, then congratulate yourself. But do you also know what *Stegosaurus* used its row of plates for?

Like most of its duckbill relatives, *Saurolophus* had an ungainly shape, making it a comparatively awkward and slow-moving dinosaur. Though many must have fallen prey to meat-eaters, duckbills as a whole thrived during the Cretaceous.

© National Museum of Natural Sciences, Ottawa, Canada/painting by Eleanor Kish

Stenonychosaurus

("Narrow-clawed lizard"). A close relative of *Saurornithoides*, this remarkable dinosaur had an even larger brain. *Stenonychosaurus* was too small (about 6 feet [1.8 meters] in length) and too slightly built to attack larger creatures, but it probably was a very successful hunter of small mammals and lizards.

Struthiosaurus

("Ostrich lizard"). No relation to the ostrich dinosaurs, this little ankylosaur was one of the few dinosaurs you might have wanted to take home as a pet. Only 6 feet (1.8 meters) long, it may have lived only on islands (where limits of food sources would have made small size a useful adaptation). *Struthiosaurus* wore several different types of armor, including long shoulder spines, bony plates on the neck, and small spines on the sides and tail.

Styracosaurus

("Spiked lizard"). With a single long horn sticking up from its nose (and twisting horns above its eyes), this 18-foot (5.5-meter) ceratopsian more than made up for its lack of weapons with an amazing neck frill. While most horned dinosaurs had relatively unadorned frills, *Styracosaurus'* featured six long spines aimed over its back. These spines might have helped convince local predators that *Styracosaurus* was a meal not worth trying for.

Supersaurus

("Super lizard"). This is a real dinosaur, although its name will probably eventually be changed. First discovered in 1972, this sauropod was at the time the largest dinosaur ever found. It apparently spanned more than 90 feet (27 meters), and stood more than 50 feet (15 meters) high. Its neck alone was nearly 40 feet (12 meters) in length, and a single vertebra measured 5 feet (1.5 meters).

Tenontosaurus

("Sinew lizard"). A fascinatingly unusual iguanodon or hypsilophodon, *Tenontosaurus* lived in Early Cretaceous western North America. It had one of the finest tails in the dinosaur universe, a tail that took up perhaps two-thirds of its 21-foot (6.5-meter) length. It also had much longer front legs than many similar dinosaurs, leading scientists to think that it may have spent much of its time walking on all fours.

Tenontosaurus bones have frequently been found in the same fossil beds as those of *Deinonychus*, the "terrible claw." This means one of two things: Either *Tenontosaurus* was a favorite prey of *Deinonychus*, or the species just shared the same habitat, and their bones ended up in the same sites.

Therizinosaurus ("Scythe lizard").

Remember *Deinocheirus*, known from only a pair of 8-foot (2.5-meter) arms tipped with claws like curved butcher's knives? Well, here's another Mongolian monstrosity, a Late Cretaceous carnosaur or deinonychosaur that also had arms measuring 8 feet (2.5 meters) in length. But *this* nightmare creature's arms were far sturdier and more massive than *Deinocheirus'*, and its curved claws—as strong and sharp as a scythe—may have measured a stunning 3 feet (92 centimeters) in length. Only if we're lucky enough to find the rest of *Therizinosaurus* will we know how this great meat-eater used its matchless weapons.

Thescelosaurus

("Wonderful lizard"). Two things distinguish this western North American dinosaur. First, it was another one of those that have proved almost impossible to classify. And second, it was one of the last dinosaurs, living at the very end of the late Cretaceous. It died out in the great extinction sixty-five million years ago.

Thescelosaurus was a mid-sized dinosaur, reaching a length of about 11 feet (3.1 meters). It had long, slender hind legs and rather strong arms, ending in five-fingered hands. It was also one of several dinosaurs equipped with bony armor, in this case chunks of bone set into the skin along its back.

Opposite page: Eye to eye with a *Triceratops*. Peaceful vegetarians they might have been, but these horned dinosaurs were as strong and as impregnable as tanks.

Triceratops

("Three-horned face"). Many groups of dinosaurs produced their largest individuals at the very end of the Late Cretaceous, right before the great extinction that doomed every last dinosaur—and the ceratopsians were no exception. There is little doubt that, at 30 feet (9 meters) in length, weighing 6 tons (5.5 metric tons), and boasting three horns that might have been 5 feet (1.5 meters) long, *Triceratops* was the most impressive of all horned dinosaurs.

Need more? Scientists now think that *Triceratops* lived and ran in huge herds. What a sight they must have made, thundering across the plains of western North America by the thousands. The whole earth would have seemed to be shaking.

Tröodon ("Wound tooth").

One of the rules of dinosaur lore is very simple: All ornithischian (bird-hipped) dinosaurs were plant-eaters. No ornithopods, boneheads, duckbills, or ankylosaurs ever touched a scrap of meat.

Enter *Tröodon*. First identified (and named) after a single, sharp, serrated tooth found in 1856, it was long thought to belong to one of the groups of meat-eating dinosaurs. Then scientists began to unearth more *Tröodon* fossils, culminating in the most complete finds yet—more teeth, jawbones, even eggs and babies discovered by John Horner and Robert Makela in 1979 and 1980.

These discoveries were remarkable, because they seemed to show that *Tröodon* was most closely related to hypsilophodons, those fast-moving dinosaurs that possessed teeth built for eating plants and plants alone. But *Tröodon*'s knifelike teeth are clearly designed for ripping flesh, so their owner may be the single exception to the grand rule: the ornithischian with a taste for meat.

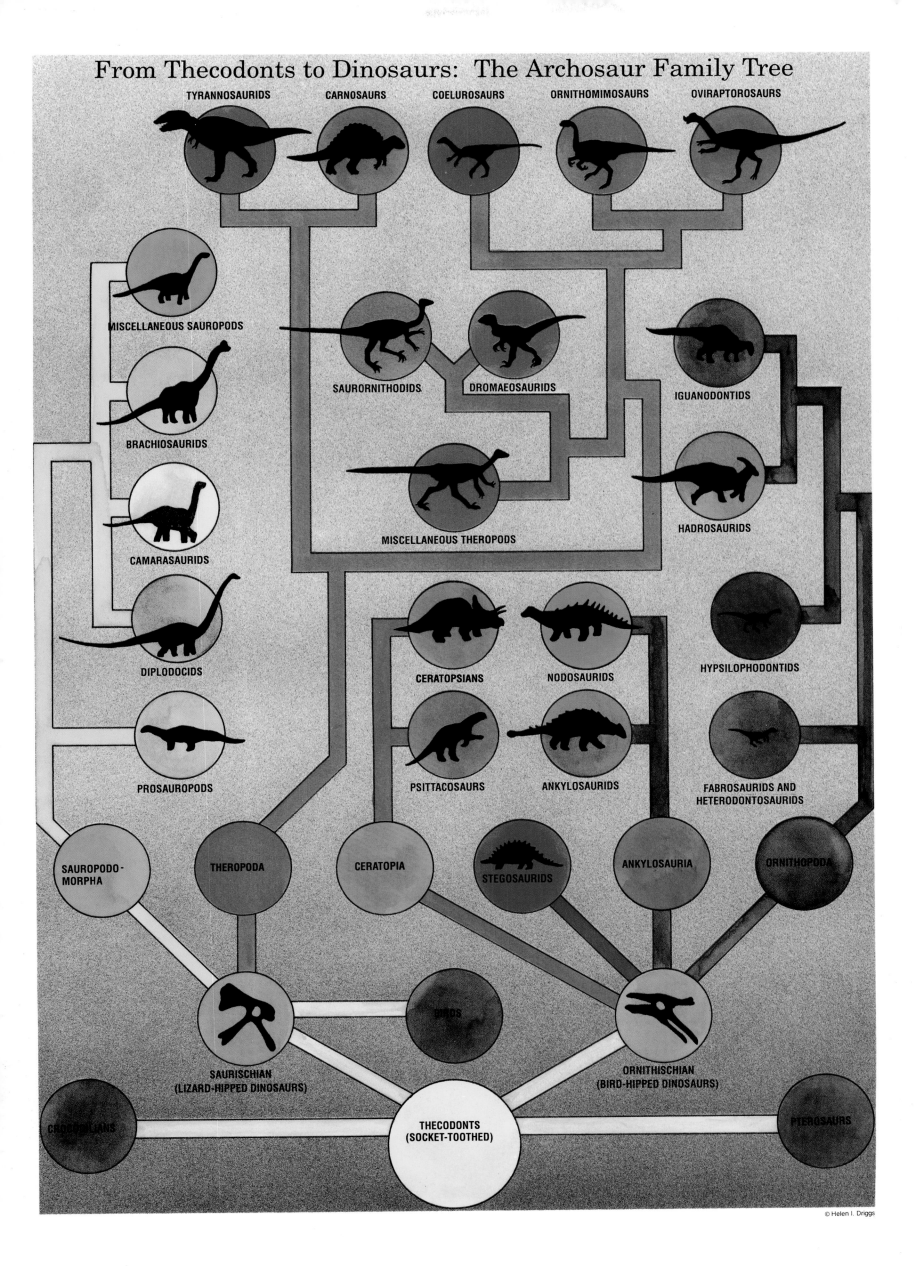

Tsintaosaurus

("Tsintao lizard"). Just when you thought you'd seen all the latest styles in duckbill headgear, here comes *Tsintaosaurus*. This 33-foot (10.2-meter) Late Cretaceous dinosaur boasted a horn that stuck straight up from the top of its head like some new-wave haircut. As in *Parasaurolophus* and others, breathing tubes ran up and back within the horn, perhaps allowing *Tsintaosaurus* to produce resonant whoops and hollers.

Few dinosaurs were more impressive—or more abundant—than the great *Triceratops*. This massive dinosaur roamed the plains of western North America during the Late Cretaceous in huge herds, driving off predators with its sword-tipped horns.

Tyrannosaurus ("Tyrant lizard"). You've waited very patiently through dinosaurs with switchblade claws, with thick heads, with new-wave horns. Now, after dozens of less important beasts, you've finally reached the section on the most popular dinosaur of all time, the great tyrant itself. And now I'm going to have to disappoint you.

Of course, at 40 or more feet (12 or more meters) in length, *Tyrannosaurus* was one of the biggest carnosaurs of all time. And no one's arguing that it didn't have a terrifyingly massive head and 7-inch (18-centimeter) teeth that looked like meat cleavers. The only question—and it's an important one—is: What did *Tyrannosaurus* do with all this weaponry?

Today, more and more scientists think that *Tyrannosaurus* was simply too large, too massive, to be an effective hunter. Instead, they believe, it stalked around its North American habitat hunting for corpses of dinosaurs that had died of natural causes. Then it would eat. Yes, *Tyrannosaurus* may have been a Late Cretaceous carrion crow, a vulture—not a slavering merchant of death.

Ultrasaurus ("Ultra lizard"). Bigger than *Apatosaurus*, more massive than *Supersaurus*, this dinosaur may have reached the remarkable length of 110 feet (34 meters), and may have weighed 150 tons (131 metric tons). When scientists get around to studying and describing it fully, it will undoubtedly be given a more sober name than *Ultrasaurus*.

Velociraptor ("Swift robber"). Like its larger and fiercer cousin *Deinonychus*, *Velociraptor* was a quick and agile predator, equipped with sharp teeth, sharp claws on its fingers, and a large switchblade claw on each foot. Although it probably usually chased after relatively small prey, in 1971 scientists found a *Velociraptor* fossil locked in an eternal embrace with a *Protoceratops*. Apparently the hunter had attacked and disemboweled the horned dinosaur. But somehow the *Protoceratops* managed to crush the *Velociraptor*'s chest at the same time, and the two dinosaurs died together.

From this *Apatosaurus* through *Velociraptor* and beyond, the dinosaurs will always capture our imaginations. (following page)

© Doug Henderson

Bibliography

Bakker, Robert T., *The Dinosaur Heresies: Unlocking the Mystery of the Dinosaurs and Their Extinction*. New York: William Morrow, 1986.

Benton, Michael, *The Dinosaur Encyclopedia*. New York: Simon and Schuster, 1984.

Brosnan, John, *Future Tense: The Cinema of Science Fiction*. New York: St. Martin's, 1978.

Charig, Alan, *A New Look at the Dinosaurs*. New York: Facts on File, 1983.

Dixon, Dougal, *The New Dinosaurs*. Salem, Massachusetts: Salem House, 1988.

Dixon, Dougal, Cox, Barry, R.J.G. Savage and Brian Gardiner, *Dinosaurs and Prehistoric Animals*. New York: Macmillan Publishing Company, 1988.

Gross, Renie, *Dinosaur Country*. Saskatoon, Saskatchewan: Western Producer Prairie Books, 1985.

Horner, John R. and Gorman, James, *Digging Dinosaurs*. New York: Workman Publishing Company, 1988.

Lambert, David, *A Field Guide to Dinosaurs*. New York: Avon, 1983.

_____, *A Field Guide to Prehistoric Life*. New York: Facts on File, 1985.

McLoughlin, John C., *Archosauria: A New Look at the Old Dinosaur*. New York: Viking, 1979.

Paul, Gregory S., *Predatory Dinosaurs of the World*. New York: Simon and Schuster, 1988.

Thompson, Ida, *The Audubon Society Field Guide to North American Fossils*. New York: Alfred A. Knopf, 1982.

Wilford, John Noble, *The Riddle of the Dinosaur*. New York: Alfred A. Knopf, 1985.